BOOK SIX

CONTENTS

Hooked On Phonics®

Copyright © 1984, 1986, 1988, 1991, 1992, 1993, 1999
Gateway Learning Corporation, 7th Edition

Printed in the United States of America.

Call 1-800-ABCDEFG®

1

2

READ OUT LOUD!

Blue  Cards

READ OUT LOUD!
- SOUNDING OUT WORDS -

able
1 **able**
2 **uble**
3 **trust able**
1 ①

© 1993

1	trust<u>able</u>	comfort<u>able</u>	reli<u>able</u>	enjoy<u>able</u>	favor<u>able</u>	li<u>able</u>
2	cap<u>able</u>	dur<u>able</u>	port<u>able</u>	soci<u>able</u>	us<u>able</u>	lov<u>able</u>
3	ador<u>able</u>	valu<u>able</u>	advis<u>able</u>	excit<u>able</u>	remov<u>able</u>	pay<u>able</u>
4	tax<u>able</u>	like<u>able</u>	size<u>able</u>	adapt<u>able</u>	agree<u>able</u>	avail<u>able</u>

al
1 **al**
2 **l**
3 **arriv al**
2 ①

© 1993

1	arriv<u>al</u>	fat<u>al</u>	brut<u>al</u>	caus<u>al</u>	natur<u>al</u>	remov<u>al</u>
2	fin<u>al</u>	leg<u>al</u>	tot<u>al</u>	tri<u>al</u>	usu<u>al</u>	voc<u>al</u>
3	ped<u>al</u>	riv<u>al</u>	soci<u>al</u>	centr<u>al</u>	etern<u>al</u>	gener<u>al</u>
4	liber<u>al</u>	form<u>al</u>	post<u>al</u>	comic<u>al</u>	ethic<u>al</u>	logic<u>al</u>
5	magic<u>al</u>	music<u>al</u>	topic<u>al</u>	trivi<u>al</u>		

READ OUT LOUD!

- REVIEW -

1	trust<u>able</u>	comfort<u>able</u>	reli<u>able</u>	enjoy<u>able</u>	favor<u>able</u>	li<u>able</u>
2	cap<u>able</u>	dur<u>able</u>	port<u>able</u>	soci<u>able</u>	us<u>able</u>	lov<u>able</u>
3	ador<u>able</u>	valu<u>able</u>	advis<u>able</u>	excit<u>able</u>	remov<u>able</u>	pay<u>able</u>
4	tax<u>able</u>	like<u>able</u>	size<u>able</u>	adapt<u>able</u>	agree<u>able</u>	avail<u>able</u>

1	arriv<u>al</u>	fat<u>al</u>	brut<u>al</u>	caus<u>al</u>	natur<u>al</u>	remov<u>al</u>
2	fin<u>al</u>	leg<u>al</u>	tot<u>al</u>	tri<u>al</u>	usu<u>al</u>	voc<u>al</u>
3	ped<u>al</u>	riv<u>al</u>	soci<u>al</u>	centr<u>al</u>	etern<u>al</u>	gener<u>al</u>
4	liber<u>al</u>	form<u>al</u>	post<u>al</u>	comic<u>al</u>	ethic<u>al</u>	logic<u>al</u>
5	magic<u>al</u>	music<u>al</u>	topic<u>al</u>	trivi<u>al</u>		

READ OUT LOUD!
- SOUNDING OUT WORDS -

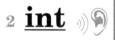

ance					
1 ins 🔊					
3 allow ance					
3 ①					

1 allowance	distance	instance	abundance	appliance	assurance
2 endurance	fragrance	ignorance	insurance	substance	brilliance
3 nuisance	clearance	acceptance	admittance	appearance	assistance
4 attendance	entrance	allegiance			

© 1993

ant					
1 int 🔊					
3 defi ant					
4 ①					

1 defiant	servant	migrant	vagrant	abundant	constant
2 dominant	fragrant	hesitant	ignorant	militant	tolerant
3 important					

© 1993

READ OUT LOUD!

- REVIEW -

1	allow<u>ance</u>	dist<u>ance</u>	inst<u>ance</u>	abund<u>ance</u>	appli<u>ance</u>	assur<u>ance</u>
2	endur<u>ance</u>	frag<u>rance</u>	igno<u>rance</u>	insur<u>ance</u>	subst<u>ance</u>	brilli<u>ance</u>
3	nuis<u>ance</u>	clear<u>ance</u>	accept<u>ance</u>	admitt<u>ance</u>	appear<u>ance</u>	assist<u>ance</u>
4	attend<u>ance</u>	ent<u>rance</u>	allegi<u>ance</u>			

1	defi<u>ant</u>	serv<u>ant</u>	mig<u>rant</u>	vag<u>rant</u>	abund<u>ant</u>	const<u>ant</u>
2	domin<u>ant</u>	frag<u>rant</u>	hesit<u>ant</u>	igno<u>rant</u>	milit<u>ant</u>	toler<u>ant</u>
3	import<u>ant</u>					

1	trustable	comfortable	reliable	enjoyable	favorable	liable	capable
2	durable	portable	sociable	usable	lovable	adorable	valuable
3	advisable	excitable	removable	payable	taxable	likeable	sizeable

READ OUT LOUD!

- REVIEW -

4	adaptable	agreeable	available	arrival	fatal	brutal	causal
5	natural	removal	final	legal	total	trial	usual
6	vocal	pedal	rival	social	central	eternal	general
7	liberal	formal	postal	comical	ethical	logical	magical
8	musical	topical	trivial				

READ OUT LOUD!
- SOUNDING OUT WORDS -

ary

1 **ary**
2 **ery** 🔊
3 legend **ary**

5 ①

© 1993

1	legend<u>ary</u>	custom<u>ary</u>	momentary secretary	diction<u>ary</u>	primary
2	imagin<u>ary</u>	contr<u>ary</u>	liter<u>ary</u> military	ordin<u>ary</u>	sanit<u>ary</u>

ate

1 **ate**
2 **at**e 🔊
3 evalu **ate**

6 ①

© 1993

1	evalu<u>ate</u>	prim<u>ate</u>	puls<u>ate</u>	activ<u>ate</u>	motiv<u>ate</u> decor<u>ate</u>
2	medic<u>ate</u>				

READ OUT LOUD!
- REVIEW -

1	legend<u>ary</u>	custom<u>ary</u>	moment<u>ary</u>	secret<u>ary</u>	diction<u>ary</u>	prim<u>ary</u>
2	imagin<u>ary</u>	contr<u>ary</u>	liter<u>ary</u>	milit<u>ary</u>	ordin<u>ary</u>	sanit<u>ary</u>

1	evalu<u>ate</u>	prim<u>ate</u>	puls<u>ate</u>	activ<u>ate</u>	motiv<u>ate</u>	decor<u>ate</u>
2	medic<u>ate</u>					

1	allowance	distance	instance	abundance	appliance	assurance	endurance
2	fragrance	ignorance	insurance	substance	brilliance	nuisance	clearance
3	acceptance	admittance	appearance	assistance	attendance	entrance	allegiance
4	defiant	servant	migrant	vagrant	abundant	constant	dominant
5	fragrant	hesitant	ignorant	militant	tolerant	important	

READ OUT LOUD!
- SOUNDING OUT WORDS -

ent
1 ent
2 **ent**
3 **cli ent**
7 ①
© 1993

1	clie__nt__	ev__ent__	ag__ent__	prud__ent__	solv__ent__	resid__ent__
2	rever__ent__					

ence
1 ens
2 **ens**
3 **confer ence**
8 ①
© 1993

1	confer__ence__	exist__ence__	refer__ence__	depend__ence__	deterr__ence__	differ__ence__
2	excell__ence__	insist__ence__	occurr__ence__	prefer__ence__	prud__ence__	resid__ence__
3	rever__ence__	compet__ence__	confid__ence__			

READ OUT LOUD!
- REVIEW -

1   cli<u>ent</u>   ev<u>ent</u>   ag<u>ent</u>   prud<u>ent</u>   solv<u>ent</u>   resid<u>ent</u>

2   rever<u>ent</u>

1   confer<u>ence</u>   exist<u>ence</u>   refer<u>ence</u>   depend<u>ence</u>   deterr<u>ence</u>   differ<u>ence</u>

2   excell<u>ence</u>   insist<u>ence</u>   occurr<u>ence</u>   prefer<u>ence</u>   prud<u>ence</u>   resid<u>ence</u>

3   rever<u>ence</u>   compet<u>ence</u>   confid<u>ence</u>

1   legendary   customary   momentary   secretary   dictionary   primary   imaginary

2   contrary   literary   military   ordinary   sanitary   evaluate   primate

3   p<u>u</u>lsate   activate   motivate   decorate   medicate

READ OUT LOUD!

- SOUNDING OUT WORDS -

ic

1 ic
2 ic
3 atom ic

1

1	atom**ic**	iron**ic**	poet**ic**	class**ic**	organ**ic**	artist**ic**
2	magnet**ic**	metall**ic**	period**ic**	traff**ic**	academ**ic**	allerg**ic**
3	dynam**ic**	histor**ic**	majest**ic**	specif**ic**	terrif**ic**	alcohol**ic**
4	bas**ic**	scen**ic**	chron**ic**	athlet**ic**	Atlant**ic**	Cathol**ic**
5	cosmet**ic**	diabet**ic**	domest**ic**	dramat**ic**	volcan**ic**	

ive

1 ive
2 ive
3 act ive

1

1	act**ive**	mass**ive**	pass**ive**	posit**ive**	addict**ive**	affect**ive**
2	assert**ive**	support**ive**	combat**ive**	defect**ive**	detect**ive**	effect**ive**
3	excess**ive**	impass**ive**	invent**ive**	object**ive**	plaint**ive**	reflex**ive**
4	secret**ive**	abus**ive**	creat**ive**	negat**ive**	relat**ive**	defens**ive**
5	execut**ive**	impuls**ive**				

READ OUT LOUD!
- REVIEW -

1	atomic	ironic	poetic	classic	organic	artistic
2	magnetic	metallic	periodic	traffic	academic	allergic
3	dynamic	historic	majestic	specific	terrific	alcoholic
4	basic	scenic	chronic	athletic	Atlantic	Catholic
5	cosmetic	diabetic	domestic	dramatic	volcanic	

1	active	massive	passive	positive	addictive	affective
2	assertive	supportive	combative	defective	detective	effective
3	excessive	impassive	inventive	objective	plaintive	reflexive
4	secretive	abusive	creative	negative	relative	defensive
5	executive	impulsive				

READ OUT LOUD!

- REVIEW -

1	client	event	agent	prudent	solvent	resident	reverent
2	conference	existence	reference	dependence	deterrence	difference	excellence
3	insistence	occurrence	preference	prudence	residence	reverence	competence
4	confidence						

READ OUT LOUD!
- SOUNDING OUT WORDS -

ment

1 **ment**

2 **ment**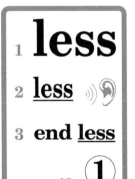

3 **pay ment**

11 ①

© 1993

1	payment	basement	movement	pavement	shipment
2	agreement	amazement	amendment	amusement	annulment
3	apartment	enjoyment	equipment	judgment	placement
4	statement	treatment	adjustment	assortment	commitment
5	department	employment	enrollment	excitement	government
6	investment	management	punishment	resentment	

less

1 **less**

2 **less**

3 **end less**

12 ①

© 1993

1	endless	godless	jobless	useless	fearless
2	harmless	helpless	homeless	lifeless	listless
3	odorless	painless	reckless	ruthless	selfless
4	spotless	timeless			

READ OUT LOUD!

- REVIEW -

1	payment	basement	movement	pavement	shipment
2	agreement	amazement	amendment	amusement	annulment
3	apartment	enjoyment	equipment	judgment	placement
4	statement	treatment	adjustment	assortment	commitment
5	department	employment	enrollment	excitement	government
6	investment	management	punishment	resentment	

1	endless	godless	jobless	useless	fearless
2	harmless	helpless	homeless	lifeless	listless
3	odorless	painless	reckless	ruthless	selfless
4	spotless	timeless			

READ OUT LOUD!
- REVIEW -

1	atomic	ironic	poetic	classic	organic	artistic	magnetic
2	metallic	periodic	traffic	academic	allergic	dynamic	historic
3	majestic	specific	terrific	alcoholic	basic	scenic	chronic
4	athletic	Atlantic	Catholic	cosmetic	diabetic	domestic	dramatic
5	volcanic	active	massive	passive	positive	addictive	affective
6	assertive	supportive	combative	defective	detective	effective	excessive
7	impassive	inventive	objective	plaintive	reflexive	secretive	abusive
8	creative	negative	relative	defensive	executive	impulsive	

READ OUT LOUD!

- SOUNDING OUT WORDS -

cious
1. **cious**
2. **shus**
3. deli **cious**

13 ①
© 1993

1	delic<u>ious</u>	grac<u>ious</u>	spac<u>ious</u>	prec<u>ious</u>	cons<u>cious</u>	fero<u>cious</u>
2	judic<u>ious</u>	tena<u>cious</u>				

ious
1. **ious**
2. **eeus**
3. glor **ious**

14 ①
© 1993

1	glor<u>ious</u>	stud<u>ious</u>	prev<u>ious</u>	hilar<u>ious</u>	labor<u>ious</u>	luxur<u>ious</u>
2	melod<u>ious</u>	notor<u>ious</u>				

READ OUT LOUD!

- REVIEW -

1	deli<u>cious</u>	gra<u>cious</u>	spa<u>cious</u>	pre<u>cious</u>	cons<u>cious</u>	fero<u>cious</u>
2	judi<u>cious</u>	tena<u>cious</u>				

1	glor<u>ious</u>	stud<u>ious</u>	previ<u>ous</u>	hilar<u>ious</u>	labor<u>ious</u>	luxur<u>ious</u>
2	melod<u>ious</u>	notor<u>ious</u>				

1	payment	basement	movement	pavement	shipment	agreement	amazement
2	amendment	amusement	annulment	apartment	enjoyment	equipment	judgment
3	placement	statement	treatment	adjustment	assortment	commitment	department
4	employment	enrollment	excitement	government	investment	management	punishment
5	resentment	endless	godless	jobless	useless	fearless	harmless
6	helpless	homeless	lifeless	listless	odorless	painless	reckless
7	ruthless	selfless	spotless	timeless			

READ OUT LOUD!
- SOUNDING OUT WORDS -

ous

1 **ous**
2 **us** 🔊
3 **joy ous**
15 ①
© 1993

1 joy<u>ous</u>	pomp<u>ous</u>	humor<u>ous</u>	peril<u>ous</u>	rigor<u>ous</u>	vigor<u>ous</u>
2 danger<u>ous</u>					

tion

1 **tion**
2 **shun** 🔊
3 **ac tion**
16 ①
© 1993

1 ac<u>tion</u>	op<u>tion</u>	elec<u>tion</u>	adop<u>tion</u>	evic<u>tion</u>	ques<u>tion</u>
2 reac<u>tion</u>	affec<u>tion</u>	deduc<u>tion</u>	dejec<u>tion</u>	diges<u>tion</u>	direc<u>tion</u>
3 excep<u>tion</u>	infec<u>tion</u>	inten<u>tion</u>	inven<u>tion</u>	objec<u>tion</u>	rejec<u>tion</u>
4 selec<u>tion</u>	pollu<u>tion</u>	promo<u>tion</u>	emo<u>tion</u>	devo<u>tion</u>	igni<u>tion</u>
5 edi<u>tion</u>	audi<u>tion</u>	posi<u>tion</u>			

READ OUT LOUD!

- REVIEW -

1	joy<u>ous</u>	pomp<u>ous</u>	humor<u>ous</u>	peril<u>ous</u>	rigor<u>ous</u>	vigor<u>ous</u>
2	danger<u>ous</u>					

1	a<u>ction</u>	op<u>tion</u>	elec<u>tion</u>	adop<u>tion</u>	evic<u>tion</u>	ques<u>tion</u>
2	rea<u>ction</u>	affec<u>tion</u>	deduc<u>tion</u>	dejec<u>tion</u>	diges<u>tion</u>	direc<u>tion</u>
3	excep<u>tion</u>	infec<u>tion</u>	inten<u>tion</u>	inven<u>tion</u>	objec<u>tion</u>	rejec<u>tion</u>
4	selec<u>tion</u>	pollu<u>tion</u>	promo<u>tion</u>	emo<u>tion</u>	devo<u>tion</u>	igni<u>tion</u>
5	edi<u>tion</u>	audi<u>tion</u>	posi<u>tion</u>			

1	delicious	gracious	spacious	precious	conscious	ferocious	judicious
2	tenacious	glorious	studious	previous	hilarious	laborious	luxurious
3	melodious	notorious					

READ OUT LOUD!

- SOUNDING OUT WORDS -

ation

1 ation

2 ashun

3 tax ation

17 ①

© 1993

1	taxation	imitation	migration	narration	operation	radiation
2	violation	creation	donation	location	relation	rotation
3	vacation	animation	dictation	education	elevation	formation
4	notation	quotation	sensation			

sion

1 sion

2 shun

3 ten sion

18 ①

© 1993

1	tension	precision	revision	confusion	recession	evasion
2	decision	delusion	division	invasion	expansion	explosion
3	extension	admission	corrosion	exclusion	persuasion	provision
4	seclusion					

READ OUT LOUD!
- REVIEW -

1	tax<u>ation</u>	imit<u>ation</u>	migr<u>ation</u>	narr<u>ation</u>	oper<u>ation</u>	radi<u>ation</u>
2	viol<u>ation</u>	cre<u>ation</u>	don<u>ation</u>	loc<u>ation</u>	rel<u>ation</u>	rot<u>ation</u>
3	vac<u>ation</u>	anim<u>ation</u>	dict<u>ation</u>	educ<u>ation</u>	elev<u>ation</u>	form<u>ation</u>
4	not<u>ation</u>	quot<u>ation</u>	sens<u>ation</u>			

1	ten<u>sion</u>	preci<u>sion</u>	revi<u>sion</u>	confu<u>sion</u>	rece<u>ssion</u>	eva<u>sion</u>
2	deci<u>sion</u>	delu<u>sion</u>	divi<u>sion</u>	inva<u>sion</u>	expan<u>sion</u>	explo<u>sion</u>
3	exten<u>sion</u>	admi<u>ssion</u>	corro<u>sion</u>	exclu<u>sion</u>	persua<u>sion</u>	provi<u>sion</u>
4	seclu<u>sion</u>					

1	joyous	pompous	humorous	perilous	rigorous	vigorous	dangerous
2	action	option	election	adoption	eviction	question	reaction

READ OUT LOUD!

- REVIEW -

3	affection	deduction	dejection	digestion	direction	exception	infection
4	intention	invention	objection	rejection	selection	pollution	promotion
5	emotion	devotion	ignition	edition	audition	position	

READ OUT LOUD!
- SOUNDING OUT WORDS -

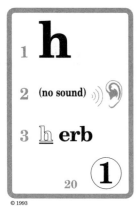

1	herb	hour	honest	honesty	honor	John
2	Buddha	Torah	shepherd	exhibit	exhibition	exhaust
3	exhausted	exhaustion	spaghetti	ghost	ghetto	honorable
4	honorary					

1	listen	depot	often	fasten	whistle	thistle
2	castle	glisten	rustle	jostle	wrestle	

28

READ OUT LOUD!
- REVIEW -

1	h̲erb	h̲our	h̲onest	h̲onesty	h̲onor	Joh̲n
2	Budd̲h̲a	Torah̲	sheph̲erd	exh̲ibit	exh̲ibition	exh̲aust
3	exh̲austed	exh̲austion	spag̲h̲etti	g̲h̲ost	g̲h̲etto	h̲onorable
4	h̲onorary					

1	lis̲t̲en	depo̲t̲	of̲t̲en	fas̲t̲en	whis̲t̲le	this̲t̲le
2	cas̲t̲le	glis̲t̲en	rus̲t̲le	jos̲t̲le	wres̲t̲le	

1	taxation	imitation	migration	narration	operation	radiation	violation
2	creation	donation	location	relation	rotation	vacation	animation
3	dictation	education	elevation	formation	notation	quotation	sensation
4	tension	precision	revision	confusion	recession	evasion	decision

READ OUT LOUD!

- REVIEW -

5	delusion	division	invasion	expansion	explosion	extension	admission

6	corrosion	exclusion	persuasion	provision	seclusion

READ OUT LOUD!
- REVIEW -

1	trustable	arrival	allowance	defiant	legendary	evaluate	client
2	conference	atomic	active	payment	endless	delicious	glorious
3	joyous	action	taxation	tension	herb	listen	comfortable
4	fatal	distance	servant	customary	primate	event	existence
5	ironic	massive	basement	godless	pompous	option	imitation
6	precision	hour	depot	reliable	brutal	instance	migrant
7	momentary	pulsate	agent	reference	poetic	passive	movement
8	jobless	gracious	studious	humorous	election	migration	revision
9	honest	often	enjoyable	causal	abundance	vagrant	secretary
10	activate	prudent	dependence	classic	positive	pavement	useless
11	spacious	previous	perilous	adoption	narration	confusion	honesty
12	fasten	favorable	natural	appliance	abundant	dictionary	motivate

READ OUT LOUD!

- REVIEW -

13	solvent	deterrence	organic	addictive	shipment	fearless	precious
14	hilarious	rigorous	eviction	operation	recession	honor	whistle
15	liable	removal	assurance	constant	primary	decorate	resident
16	difference	artistic	affective	agreement	harmless	conscious	laborious
17	vigorous	question	radiation	evasion	John	thistle	capable
18	final	endurance	dominant	imaginary	medicate	reverent	excellence
19	magnetic	assertive	amazement	helpless	ferocious	luxurious	dangerous
20	reaction	violation	decision	Buddha	castle	durable	legal
21	fragrance	fragrant	contrary	insistence	metallic	supportive	amendment
22	homeless	judicious	melodious	affection	creation	delusion	Torah
23	glisten	portable	total	ignorance	hesitant	literary	occurrence
24	periodic	combative	amusement	lifeless	tenacious	notorious	deduction

READ OUT LOUD!

- REVIEW -

25	donation	division	shepherd	rustle	sociable	trial	insurance
26	ignorant	military	preference	traffic	defective	annulment	listless
27	dejection	location	invasion	exhibit	jostle	usable	usual
28	substance	militant	ordinary	prudence	academic	detective	apartment
29	odorless	digestion	relation	expansion	exhibition	wrestle	lovable
30	vocal	brilliance	tolerant	sanitary	residence	allergic	effective
31	enjoyment	painless	direction	rotation	explosion	exhaust	adorable
32	pedal	nuisance	important	reverence	dynamic	excessive	equipment
33	reckless	exception	vacation	extension	exhausted	valuable	rival
34	clearance	competence	historic	impassive	judgment	ruthless	infection
35	animation	admission	exhaustion	advisable	social	acceptance	confidence
36	majestic	inventive	placement	selfless	intention	dictation	corrosion

READ OUT LOUD!

- REVIEW -

37	spaghetti	excitable	central	admittance	specific	objective	statement
38	invention	education	exclusion	ghost	removable	eternal	appearance
39	terrific	plaintive	treatment	spotless	objection	elevation	persuasion
40	ghetto	payable	general	assistance	alcoholic	reflexive	adjustment
41	timeless	rejection	formation	provision	honorable	taxable	liberal
42	attendance	basic	secretive	assortment	selection	notation	seclusion
43	honorary	likeable	formal	entrance	scenic	abusive	commitment
44	pollution	quotation	sizeable	postal	allegiance	chronic	creative
45	department	promotion	sensation	adaptable	comical	athletic	negative
46	employment	emotion	agreeable	ethical	Atlantic	relative	enrollment
47	devotion	available	logical	Catholic	defensive	excitement	ignition
48	magical	edition	musical	audition	topical	government	position

READ OUT LOUD!

- REVIEW -

49	investment	trivial	cosmetic	executive	management	diabetic	impulsive
50	punishment	domestic	resentment	dramatic	volcanic		

READ BOOK

Hooked On Phonics®
Reading Review Book

⑦

Gateway Learning Corporation • 1-800-ABCDEFG®

Pages 3–123

READ OUT LOUD!

Blue  *Cards*

2

READ OUT LOUD!
- SOUNDING OUT WORDS -

ian
1 **ian**
2 **eeun**
3 **guard ian**
1 ②
© 1993

1 guardian	median	ruffian	Canadian	meridian	amphibian
2 barbarian	custodian	pedestrian	vegetarian	Iranian	Bostonian
3 comedian					

eon
1 **eon**
2 **in**
3 **surg eon**
2 ②
© 1993

1 surgeon   pigeon   dungeon   bludgeon   luncheon

READ OUT LOUD!
- REVIEW -

1	guard<u>ian</u>	med<u>ian</u>	ruff<u>ian</u>	Canad<u>ian</u>	merid<u>ian</u>	amphib<u>ian</u>
2	barbar<u>ian</u>	custod<u>ian</u>	pedestr<u>ian</u>	vegetar<u>ian</u>	Iran<u>ian</u>	Boston<u>ian</u>
3	comed<u>ian</u>					

1	surg<u>eon</u>	pig<u>eon</u>	dung<u>eon</u>	bludg<u>eon</u>	lunch<u>eon</u>

READ OUT LOUD!

- SOUNDING OUT WORDS -

oes

1 **oes**

2 **oz**))🕪

3 **ech oes**

③ **2**

3

© 1993

1	ech**oes**	her**oes**	hob**oes**	banj**oes**	carg**oes**	domin**oes**
2	potat**oes**	tomat**oes**	torped**oes**	volcan**oes**		

ness

1 **ness**

2 **ness**))🕪

3 **mad ness**

④ **2**

4

© 1993

1	mad**ness**	fit**ness**	ill**ness**	sad**ness**	bold**ness**	damp**ness**
2	dark**ness**	fair**ness**	kind**ness**	like**ness**	neat**ness**	rude**ness**
3	sick**ness**					

READ OUT LOUD!

- REVIEW -

1 echoes   heroes   hoboes   banjoes   cargoes   dominoes

2 potatoes   tomatoes   torpedoes   volcanoes

1 madness   fitness   illness   sadness   boldness   dampness

2 darkness   fairness   kindness   likeness   neatness   rudeness

3 sickness

1 guardian   median   ruffian   Canadian   meridian   amphibian   barbarian

2 custodian   pedestrian   vegetarian   Iranian   Bostonian   comedian   surgeon

3 pigeon   dungeon   bludgeon   luncheon

READ OUT LOUD!
- SOUNDING OUT WORDS -

ish

1 **ish**

2 **ish**))

3 **Brit ish**

5 **②**

© 1993

1	British	boyish	Jewish	babyish	Finnish	foolish
2	girlish	hawkish	selfish	Turkish	devilish	feverish
3	Scottish	sluggish	Danish	Polish	stylish	Swedish
4	ticklish					

ion

1 **ion**

2 **yun**))

3 **opin ion**

6 **②**

© 1993

1	opinion	rebellion	communion

42

READ OUT LOUD!

- REVIEW -

1	British	boyish	Jewish	babyish	Finnish	foolish
2	girlish	hawkish	selfish	Turkish	devilish	feverish
3	Scottish	sluggish	Danish	Polish	stylish	Swedish
4	ticklish					

1	opinion	rebellion	communion

1	echoes	heroes	hoboes	banjoes	cargoes	dominoes	potatoes
2	tomatoes	torpedoes	volcanoes	madness	fitness	illness	sadness
3	boldness	dampness	darkness	fairness	kindness	likeness	neatness
4	rudeness	sickness					

READ OUT LOUD!
- SOUNDING OUT WORDS -

ch

1 **ch**
2 **sh**))🦻
3 **ch** ef

7 ②
© 1993

	1	chef	chute	chaise

ar

1 **ar**
2 **or**))🦻
3 **w ar**

8 ②
© 1993

1	war	swarm	warm	wart	quart	ward
2	award	reward	warn	quarrel	quarter	dwarf
3	warmth	quarry	wardrobe			

READ OUT LOUD!
- REVIEW -

| *1* | <u>ch</u>ef | <u>ch</u>ute | <u>ch</u>aise | | | |

1	w<u>ar</u>	sw<u>ar</u>m	w<u>ar</u>m	w<u>ar</u>t	qu<u>ar</u>t	w<u>ar</u>d
2	aw<u>ar</u>d	rew<u>ar</u>d	w<u>ar</u>n	qu<u>ar</u>rel	qu<u>ar</u>ter	dw<u>ar</u>f
3	w<u>ar</u>mth	qu<u>ar</u>ry	w<u>ar</u>drobe			

1	British	boyish	Jewish	babyish	Finnish	foolish	girlish
2	hawkish	selfish	Turkish	devilish	feverish	Scottish	sluggish
3	Danish	Polish	stylish	Swedish	ticklish	opinion	rebellion
4	communion						

READ OUT LOUD!

- SOUNDING OUT WORDS -

rh

1. **rh**
2. **r**h
3. **rh** ino
9 ②
© 1993

1   <u>rh</u>ino   <u>rh</u>ythm   <u>rh</u>umba   <u>rh</u>apsody   <u>Rh</u>oda

---

ei

1. **ei**
2. **a**
3. **v ei n**
10 ②
© 1993

1   v<u>ei</u>n   r<u>ei</u>n   v<u>ei</u>l   f<u>ei</u>nt

READ OUT LOUD!
- REVIEW -

| *1* | rhino | rhythm | rhumba | rhapsody | Rhoda | | |

| *1* | vein | rein | veil | feint | | | |

1	chef	chute	chaise	war	swarm	warm	wart
2	quart	ward	award	reward	warn	quarrel	quarter
3	dwarf	warmth	quarry	wardrobe			

READ OUT LOUD!

- SOUNDING OUT WORDS -

olt

1 **olt**

2 **olt**

3 **c olt**

11 ②

© 1993

1   c<u>olt</u>   b<u>olt</u>   j<u>olt</u>   v<u>olt</u>   b<u>olt</u>ing   j<u>olt</u>ing

---

ild

1 **ild**

2 **ild**

3 **w ild**

12 ②

© 1993

1   w<u>ild</u>   m<u>ild</u>   ch<u>ild</u>   m<u>ild</u>ness

READ OUT LOUD!
- REVIEW -

1 c<u>olt</u>   b<u>olt</u>   j<u>olt</u>   v<u>olt</u>   b<u>olt</u>ing   j<u>olt</u>ing

1 w<u>ild</u>   m<u>ild</u>   ch<u>ild</u>   m<u>ild</u>ness

1 rhino   rhythm   rhumba   rhapsody   Rhoda   vein   rein

2 veil   feint

READ OUT LOUD!

- SOUNDING OUT WORDS -

iest
1 iest
2 eeist
3 stick iest
13 ②
© 1993

1	stick<u>iest</u>	smell<u>iest</u>	smogg<u>iest</u>	snobb<u>iest</u>	spunk<u>iest</u>	stink<u>iest</u>
2	stuff<u>iest</u>	string<u>iest</u>	scratch<u>iest</u>	trash<u>iest</u>	trend<u>iest</u>	trick<u>iest</u>
3	filth<u>iest</u>					

ism
1 ism
2 izm
3 bapt ism
14 ②
© 1993

1	bapt<u>ism</u>	ego<u>ism</u>	rac<u>ism</u>	pr<u>ism</u>	hero<u>ism</u>	Juda<u>ism</u>
2	Marx<u>ism</u>	real<u>ism</u>	tour<u>ism</u>	Commun<u>ism</u>		

READ OUT LOUD!
- REVIEW -

1	stick<u>iest</u>	smell<u>iest</u>	smogg<u>iest</u>	snobb<u>iest</u>	spunk<u>iest</u>	stink<u>iest</u>
2	stuff<u>iest</u>	string<u>iest</u>	scratch<u>iest</u>	trash<u>iest</u>	trend<u>iest</u>	trick<u>iest</u>
3	filth<u>iest</u>					

1	bapt<u>ism</u>	ego<u>ism</u>	rac<u>ism</u>	pr<u>ism</u>	hero<u>ism</u>	Juda<u>ism</u>
2	Marx<u>ism</u>	real<u>ism</u>	tour<u>ism</u>	Commun<u>ism</u>		

1	colt	bolt	jolt	volt	bolting	jolting	wild
2	mild	child	mildness				

READ OUT LOUD!

- SOUNDING OUT WORDS -

ugh

1 **ugh**

2 **f**

3 la **ugh**

15 ②

© 1993

1   laugh   rough   cough   enough

ould

1 **ould**

2 **ood**
(good)

3 c **ould**

16 ②

© 1993

1   could   would   should   couldn't   wouldn't   shouldn't

READ OUT LOUD!
- REVIEW -

1   la<u>ugh</u>   ro<u>ugh</u>   co<u>ugh</u>   eno<u>ugh</u>

1   c<u>ou</u>ld   w<u>ou</u>ld   sh<u>ou</u>ld   c<u>ou</u>ldn't   w<u>ou</u>ldn't   sh<u>ou</u>ldn't

1   stickiest   smelliest   smoggiest   snobbiest   spunkiest   stinkiest   stuffiest

2   stringiest   scratchiest   trashiest   trendiest   trickiest   filthiest   baptism

3   egoism   racism   prism   heroism   Judaism   Marxism   realism

4   tourism   Communism

READ OUT LOUD!
- SOUNDING OUT WORDS -

et

1 **et**

2 **a**

3 **buff et**

17 **②**

© 1993

1   buff<u>et</u>   fil<u>et</u>   val<u>et</u>   ball<u>et</u>   ber<u>et</u>

---

mn

1 **mn**

2 **mn**

3 **hy mn**

18 **②**

© 1993

1   hy<u>mn</u>   autu<u>mn</u>   colu<u>mn</u>   sole<u>mn</u>   conde<u>mn</u>

READ OUT LOUD!
- REVIEW -

1 buff<u>et</u>   fil<u>et</u>   val<u>et</u>   ball<u>et</u>   ber<u>et</u>

1 hy<u>mn</u>   autu<u>mn</u>   colu<u>mn</u>   sole<u>mn</u>   conde<u>mn</u>

1 laugh   rough   cough   enough   could   would   should

2 couldn't   wouldn't   shouldn't

READ OUT LOUD!
- SOUNDING OUT WORDS -

1	piano	visa	kilo	Lisa	mini	liter
2	Miami	ravine	pizza	tiara	viola	axiom
3	chili	chino	idiom	idiot	magazine	gasoline
4	ski	police	trio	patio	deli	

1	guilt	guile	guide	guest	guard	league
2	vague	guild	guitar	guilty		

56

READ OUT LOUD!

- REVIEW -

1	piano	visa	kilo	Lisa	mini	liter
2	Miami	ravine	pizza	tiara	viola	axiom
3	chili	chino	idiom	idiot	magazine	gasoline
4	ski	police	trio	patio	deli	

1	guilt	guile	guide	guest	guard	league
2	vague	guild	guitar	guilty		

1	buffet	filet	valet	ballet	beret	hymn	autumn
2	column	solemn	condemn				

READ OUT LOUD!

- REVIEW -

1	guardian	surgeon	echoes	madness	British	opinion	chef
2	war	rhino	vein	trio	colt	wild	stickiest
3	baptism	laugh	could	buffet	hymn	piano	guilt
4	median	pigeon	heroes	fitness	boyish	rebellion	chute
5	swarm	rhythm	rein	bolt	mild	smelliest	egoism
6	rough	would	filet	autumn	visa	guile	ruffian
7	dungeon	hoboes	illness	Jewish	communion	chaise	warm
8	rhumba	veil	jolt	child	smoggiest	racism	cough
9	police	should	boldness	column	kilo	guide	Canadian
10	bludgeon	banjoes	sadness	babyish	wart	deli	rhapsody
11	feint	volt	mildness	scratchiest	prism	enough	couldn't
12	valet	solemn	Lisa	guest	patio	meridian	luncheon
13	cargoes	dampness	Finnish	quart	magazine	ticklish	gasoline

READ OUT LOUD!
- REVIEW -

14	Rhoda	bolting	snobbiest	heroism	wouldn't	ballet	condemn
15	mini	guard	amphibian	dominoes	darkness	foolish	ward
16	jolting	spunkiest	Judaism	shouldn't	beret	liter	league
17	barbarian	ski	potatoes	fairness	girlish	award	stinkiest
18	Marxism	Miami	vague	custodian	tomatoes	kindness	hawkish
19	reward	stuffiest	realism	ravine	guild	pedestrian	torpedoes
20	likeness	selfish	warn	stringiest	tourism	pizza	guitar
21	vegetarian	volcanoes	neatness	Turkish	quarrel	trashiest	Communism
22	tiara	guilty	Iranian	rudeness	devilish	quarter	trickiest
23	viola	Bostonian	sickness	feverish	dwarf	trendiest	axiom
24	comedian	Scottish	warmth	filthiest	chili	sluggish	quarry
25	chino	Danish	idiom	Polish	wardrobe	stylish	idiot
26	Swedish						

READ BOOK

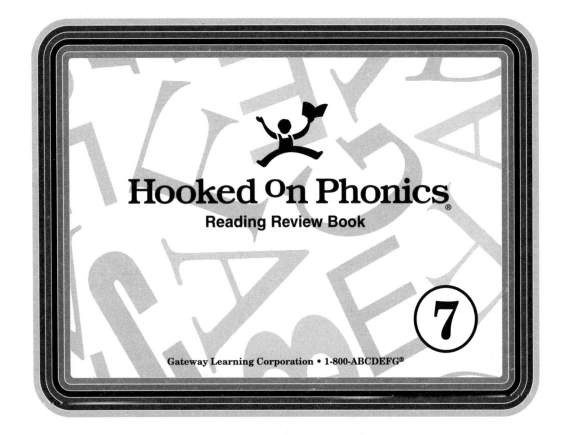

Hooked On Phonics

Reading Review Book

⑦

Gateway Learning Corporation • 1-800-ABCDEFG®

Pages 3–130